THE DOMINIE WOR

Bird Families & Life Cycles

GRAHAM MEADOWS & CLAIRE VIAL

Contents

DOMINIE PRESS
Pearson Learning Group

North American
wood ducks

 # Raising a Family

To raise a family, birds need to

find a partner,

locate a safe place to nest,

Marabou storks

gather nest material to build a nest,

A red-winged starling

and feed and raise their young.

A common coot feeds her young.

incubate the eggs,

A brolga crane

lay eggs,

A blackbird with eggs

3

Finding a Partner

Most birds **mate** during a particular time of the year, usually in spring.

In most bird **species**, the male **courts** the female. To attract a female, the male may use feather displays, songs, body movements, or even gifts of food.

Feather Displays
In many bird species, the male is more brightly colored than the female. During the **breeding season**, some males display their colorful feathers to attract females.

Songs
In many songbirds, females are attracted to the males that sing the loudest, longest, or most varied songs.

A male yellow-rumped widow sings its song.

A male sulphur-crested cockatoo raises the crest of feathers on its head to display to a female.

To attract a female, a peacock displays its brightly colored tail feathers.

In a few bird species, such as painted button-quails, the female displays to the male.

A Brahminy myna

5

Body Movements

Body movements include bowing, nodding, dancing, and raising and flapping wings.

Other Ways of Attracting a Female

Male weaverbirds build a nest to attract a female. If a female likes the nest, she will move in and lay her eggs.

Some male birds offer food to a female as a gift.

Male great frigatebirds have a bright red neck pouch. They inflate the pouch to attract a female.

Male and female Australasian gannets touch bills during courtship.

To attract a female, a male white stork holds out its wings and moves its head up and down.

6

A male masked weaver builds a nest.

A male great frigatebird inflates its pouch.

A male white-fronted tern offers fish to a female.

Java sparrows

Staying Together

The length of time a male and female bird stay together varies among species.

Forming a Pair
In many bird species, such as the Java sparrow, the male and female stay together for only one season.

In some bird species, such as Hawaiian geese and zebra finches, the male and female stay together for life.

Forming Flocks
Some bird species, such as the domestic chicken, form **flocks**. The males and females stay together all year round. One male courts and mates with more than one female.

Male and female Hawaiian geese walk with their goslings, or baby geese.

This is a sulphur-crested cockatoo, which breeds in the hollow limbs or trunks of trees.

8

These zebra finches are beginning to build a nest.

Rooster with three hens

9

This white-faced owl is nesting inside a hollow tree.

Building a Nest

Most birds build nests. A nest helps to protect the eggs and keep them warm. Some birds, such as ducks, nest alone. Others, such as terns, nest together in **colonies**.

Who Builds the Nest?

In many bird species, the male and the female build the nest. In some species, such as weaverbirds, the male builds the nest. In others, such as grouse, the female builds the nest.

Materials for the Nest

Most birds collect material to build a nest. Nest material includes branches, grass, mud, moss, feathers, and even pieces of plastic.

Most birds build a new nest each year.

This welcome swallow's nest is made of mud and lined with feathers.

These masked plovers are nesting on the ground.

White-fronted terns nesting in a colony on a cliff.

This yellow-billed spoonbill is nesting high up in a tree.

11

Female mallard ducks cover their eggs when they leave their nest.

Laying Eggs

All birds lay eggs. The number of eggs laid varies among species. For example, the kiwi lays one egg, whereas the mallard may lay ten or more. A group of eggs in a nest is called a **clutch**.

Eggs vary in size among different species. The ostrich lays the largest egg, weighing about three and a half pounds. Hummingbirds lay the smallest eggs, weighing about one-fifth of an ounce.

Eggs vary in color. The colors include white, blue, and brown. The eggs of ground-nesting birds are often dark-colored, with **speckles** that help to **camouflage** them.

A clutch of ostrich eggs

A clutch of masked plover eggs in a nest on the ground

The eggs of a song thrush are light blue, with a few black speckles.

Some cuckoos lay their eggs in the nests of other birds.

A fantail incubating its eggs

Incubation

Most birds sit on their eggs to provide warmth. This is called incubation.

In some species, such as the fantail, the male and the female take turns incubating their eggs. In a few species, such as the emu, only the male incubates the eggs.

The length of time a bird incubates its eggs varies among species.

Some species, such as brush turkeys, build large mounds of plant material in which to lay their eggs. The warmth inside the mound incubates the eggs.

Peaceful doves incubate their eggs for about fourteen days.

A brush turkey nest

White storks incubate their eggs for thirty-three to thirty-four days.

The eggs of some endangered species, such as the New Zealand kiwi, are collected and hatched in incubators.

Hatching

Most baby birds have a special **egg tooth** on the end of their beak. When a baby bird is ready to hatch, it uses the egg tooth to break open the egg shell. The egg tooth falls off soon after the **chick**, or baby bird, has hatched.

A young house sparrow

Baby kiwis do not have an egg tooth. They use their long beak and large feet to break open the eggshell.

A kiwi chick

A Duckling Hatches

A small hole appears in the egg.

The duckling, or baby duck, is using its beak to break open the shell.

The duckling starts to wriggle out of the eggshell.

The wet duckling is drying off.

The duckling's soft down feathers are now dry.

Emu chicks

These blackbird chicks are one day old.

Baby Birds

Some chicks hatch out with soft downy feathers. They can follow their parents around and find their own food shortly after hatching. Most of these species nest on the ground. Examples include emus and pheasants.

Some chicks hatch out without feathers. Their eyes are closed, and they depend on their parents for food and warmth. Most of these species nest in trees. Examples include blackbirds and robins.

A baby chicken

A black swan watches over her cygnets, or baby swans.

Emperor penguin chicks hatch with soft downy feathers, but they depend on their parents for food and warmth.

A male blackbird feeds its chicks.

 # Growing Up and Leaving the Nest

Chicks that hatch without feathers stay in the nest until they have grown their feathers. During this time, one or both of their parents feed them. The length of time a chick stays in its nest varies among species. For example, blackbird chicks stay in the nest for about two weeks.

A chick that has not left the nest is called a **nestling**.

Once a chick has left its nest, it is called a **fledgling**. In most species, the fledgling's parents keep an eye on it while it is learning to fly and feed itself. The length of time the parents look after their fledglings varies among species.

The parents of this fledgling house sparrow will look after it for several days.

This peaceful dove nestling (on the right) is almost ready to leave its nest.

The birds build a
nest in a colony.

The female gannet
lays an egg.

The birds
gather material
for their nest.

A male and female
come together and
touch bills to bond.

The Life Cycle of a Gannet

Gannets nest in colonies. The female lays just
one egg. Both parents feed the growing chick.
The chick's down feathers are replaced by its
first adult feathers, which are gray and brown.
The parents fly away, leaving the chick alone
with no food. The chick flaps its wings to
strengthen its flight muscles. Once it takes off,
it flies away to the ocean to live and find food.
About five years later, it returns to land to find
a **mate** and raise a chick.

The birds feed their growing chick.

The chick grows its first adult feathers.

The chick is about to fly away to live on an ocean.

About five years later, the adult gannet returns to land in order to mate and raise a chick.

Glossary

breeding season: The time of year, usually spring, during which animals mate

camouflage: To blend into the immediate surroundings in order to avoid being seen by predators or prey

chick: A young bird

clutch: A group of eggs in a bird's nest

colonies: Groups of animals of the same kind that live together

court (v): To behave in a way that is intended to attract another animal of the same species in order to mate

egg tooth: A hard, sharp point on the beak of an unhatched bird that is used to break through the eggshell

fledgling: A young bird that has recently left its nest

flocks: Groups of birds of the same kind that live together

incubate: To keep an egg warm until it is ready to hatch

mate (n): Either member of a pair of animals of the same species engaged in breeding

mate (v): To join with another animal of the same species in order to produce offspring

nestling: A young bird that has not left its nest

species: A group of animals or plants that have many physical characteristics in common

speckles: Small discolorations or spots

Index